Because
I CARE

A CAREGIVERS JOURNAL

Because I Care: A Care Giver's Journal

Printed in the United States of America First Printing
ISBN 978-1-955148-40-5 (pbk)
A2Z Books Publishing Lithonia, GA 30058
www.A2ZBookspublishing.net

Manufactured in the United States of America.
A2Z Books Publishing has allowed this work to remain exactly as
the authorintended, verbatim.

This Journal Belongs To

Dear Caregiver...

In 2020 my husband and I became fulltime care givers to a loved one with Dementia. Her spouse had a stroke and two months later was stricken with COVID-19 and did not make it. Like a lot of people 2020 for us was clearly a year of change and growth.

Becoming fulltime caregivers to an adult parent is the hardest thing either of us has ever experienced. To watch your loved one go through a debilitating disease right before you is very overwhelming. Dementia like other diseases is not kind. Your loved one is in a constant state of confusion and they don't understand what is happening. I know many of you have different situations that has caused you to be a caregiver and I want you to know that you are appreciated. Remember it is an illness that no one has control over.

Thank you for choosing this journal. I decided to create this journal because journaling helped me to keep my sanity through this process. I needed a safe place to express my feelings without the fear of judgement. I needed away to step away from the many titles I carry and just focus on me: not my husband, not family or anyone else who may have been monitoring or watching the situation unfold. So, throughout the pages you will find words of encouragement and support. I have written letters to share more about my journey and what I experienced in hopes that you find comfort in knowing you are not alone.

Praying that this brings you comfort, peace and a great story to share when the time is right. Good luck to you and know that you are amazing!

Because I Care

Because I care

You are doing a great job!

Because I care

You are doing a great job!

Because I care

You are doing a great job!

Because I care

You are doing a great job!

Because I care

You are doing a great job!

Because I care

You are doing a great job!

Dear Caregiver,

It was not a good day today. I woke up to get my coffee and start a little meditation before work. I went to the kitchen and it is dark as it normally is as 6:00 am. To my surprise, when I turned on the light, I realized that someone was in the dark quietly trying to sneak cereal. She was surprised when the lights went on. She said Ut OH, I'm caught with a little giggle.

I tried to smile and seem unbothered, but I know my body language was stiff. I started moving quickly so I can avoid the conversation and trying to cover the fact that I was annoyed. Nothing is wrong with her eating or feeding herself, because it is one less thing for us to worry about. However, getting up at this time before work and facing the day is so important and it had been interrupted at 6:00 am.

I'm so grateful for my journal. It is a safe place to express my feelings. Remember no matter what your loved one is faced with its ok for you to want time for yourself and it is ok to take time for yourself. You cannot care for others when you have not recharged by caring for yourself.

Because I care

Because I care

You are doing a great job!

Because I care

JOURNAL YOUR FEELINGS

You are doing a great job!

Because I care

You are doing a great job!

Because I care

You are doing a great job!

Because I care

You are doing a great job!

Because I care

You are doing a great job!

Dear Caregiver,

It's only been a few weeks since our loved one moved in. I find that I just need to vent sometimes otherwise I might just lose my mind. I can't watch TV in my room with my door closed. She came in and said, turn it down at 9:30 p.m. Urgh! Today my son is in his room having a private conversation with someone on the phone and used a 4-letter word. She starts yelling at him and then tells me he should respect others in the house. My reaction was you should respect others as well. He is having a private conversation and he is an adult, you can't tell him how to speak..

This is so distributing to me because she sits in silence listening to everything that happens in the house. She even told my husband that she knows everything happening in our house.

I share this with you because I know you are experiencing something like this. I will say that it felt really bad at the time it was happening to me. But in hindsight, we are all ok and you will be ok too. Sending hugs and remember you are not alone in this journey. Be encouraged, my friend.

Because I Care

Because I care

JOURNAL YOUR FEELINGS

You are doing a great job!

Because I care

You are doing a great job!

Because I care

You are doing a great job!

Because I care

JOURNAL YOUR FEELINGS

You are doing a great job!

Because I care

You are doing a great job!

Because I care

You are doing a great job!

Dear Caregiver,

It's been a few months now and I decided that I should take a look at a few websites to see what support is available. I was amazed at all the resources and recommendations they offered. I just need a way to manage my stress level. I don't even know what that looks like. How do I communicate and get space with my husband? How do you help yourself first?

I feel like I'm on an airplane and the oxygen mask has dropped down. My instinct is to help my husband first, but I'm gasping for air myself. How do I help him and save myself too? I can't imagine what he is feeling right now. If I feel like I can't breathe has he just stopped breathing...? This disease is not fair. It is heart breaking and hurtful. You want to do your best to take care of your family member but it is so hard. I find myself angry because I don't have control.

I can't even wash the dishes without a fight. I never thought I would care about washing the dishes. This is crazy! We are in the middle of a pandemic and I'm working every day at home now. Ideally this would-be great right? Wake up 30 minutes before you start work, log in and have a great day. Well, that is not my story. I have someone going outside a couple of times a day to look for her car. A car she has not driven in over 10 years. Every car is her car. Yesterday I went to get in my car to take my drive to the coffee shop, just so I could just breathe for a moment and to my surprise she had put her purse and her bible in my car because she said it was her car. It made me chuckle and made me cry all in the same few minutes.

You are ok, dont let the little things take a way your joy. Remember they love you and really wouldnt do these things if they could remember or if they could take care of themselves. No matter the illness the confusion, the anger and sadness is normal. Just love on them for as long as you can.

Because I care

Because I care

You are doing a great job!

Because I care

You are doing a great job!

Because I care

You are doing a great job!

Because I care

You are doing a great job!

Because I care

JOURNAL YOUR FEELINGS

You are doing a great job!

Because I care

You are doing a great job!

Dear Caregiver...

Today was a better day. Mom slept in today. No activity downstairs until late afternoon. I went up to check on her and you know she had found a suitcase and tried to put all her clothes on the hangers in her bag so she could go home. She packed up things from her drawers and said it was time for her to go.

She brought the bag down to the front door and got her coat. She told me she was waiting for her ride to come and get her. The first few times this happened I tried really hard to explain that she lived here, and this was her home now.

This time I just said OK let me know before you leave. !

I hope you have a great day! Every day will not be a bad day. Find the humor wherever you can. Laugh at yourself and laugh with your loved one. They could use a good laugh. I'm sure.

Because I Care

Because I care

You are doing a great job!

Because I care

You are doing a great job!

Because I care

You are doing a great job!

Because I care

You are doing a great job!

Because I care

You are doing a great job!

Because I care

You are doing a great job!

Dear Caregiver,

Well today's adventure started something like this.

Mom : I don't understand what we are doing

Me : We are watching TV right now.

Mom : No. I mean I don't understand this living arrangement

Me : What do you mean, your room is right up at the top of the stairs. Are you ready for bed?

Mom : So, you mean to tell me that he just moved you into my house and I have to sleep upstairs?

At this point my husband enters the room and she says I don't understand what is going on. You just moved her in here and I have to sleep upstairs. Where do you sleep?

This was a crazy exchange that occurred. She thought her son was her husband and I was the other women. She was not happy at all. There is more to the story but just know that this was yet another day that was difficult, but we made it through.

Know that you will make it through to another day. You are not alone and you are not being insensitive when you have an emotional reaction to things that are going on. Just know the most important thing is the safety and care of you and your family member. You got this!!

Because I care

Because I care

You are doing a great job!

Because I care

You are doing a great job!

Because I care

JOURNAL YOUR FEELINGS

You are doing a great job!

Because I care

You are doing a great job!

Because I care

You are doing a great job!

Because I care

You are doing a great job!

Dear Caregiver...

We have been through a lot. From the waking up in the middle of the night to find her outside in the driveway. to the sneaking out the back door just strolling down the field that runs behind our house. to being lost in Walmart. It's been crazy.

We are searching every day for her purse she hides and then says that someone must have moved it or something. Hiding is an obsession. I believe she thinks that she is keeping it safe and can't remember where she puts things. I have spent a lot of hours looking for things. The remote control was missing for months. One day it appeared on top of the entertainment center under the flower arrangement.

Because I Care

Because I care

You are doing a great job!

Because I care

JOURNAL YOUR FEELINGS

You are doing a great job!

Because I care

JOURNAL YOUR FEELINGS

You are doing a great job!

Because I care

You are doing a great job!

Because I care

You are doing a great job!

Because I care

You are doing a great job!

Dear Caregiver...

I hope the notes along the way encouraged you and supported you. I hope it has allowed you to laugh a little and reflect a little. You are doing an amazing job and you are not alone even though it may seem that way sometimes. Continue to take time for yourself and get help when you needed it.

Because I Care

Alicia is a native Michigander. She and her husband have been gifted with 5 children and one adorable granddaughter. Professionally, Alicia has worn many hats from retail management, health care benefits administration and Business Process Outsourcing (BPO), Caregiver and is currently a Project Manager for a large utility company. She holds a BA from Davenport University and has well over 25+ years of leadership experience.

Alicia is a member of the Minority Advisory Panel (MAP) Steering Committee, where she is committed to creating a more diverse, equitable and inclusive environment, and leads the MAP Mentorship program. Alicia also serves on the board of a non-profit organization called Wake Upp, where she is able to mentor young people and give back to her community. In addition is a member of Toastmaster International Power Club.

When she is not busy with all that she is also founder of My Momma Said LLC, where she focuses her time on coaching and mentoring young people by building confidence and social awareness. Alicia has a passion for helping others achieve more.

Contact Alicia @ aroach36@gmail.com
Facebook: facebook.com/mmscoaching

Interested in Writing and/or Publishing a Book?
Contact Dr. Synovia @a2zbooksublishing.net

www.ingramcontent.com/pod-product-compliance
Lightning Source LLC
Chambersburg PA
CBHW040905120626
46551CB00006B/650